Original title:
Life's Meaning: Still Looking for the Map

Copyright © 2025 Creative Arts Management OÜ
All rights reserved.

Author: Thomas Sinclair
ISBN HARDBACK: 978-1-80566-294-5
ISBN PAPERBACK: 978-1-80566-589-2

Whispers of the Wind's Direction

The compass spins, round and round,
It points to the snacks I just found.
Clouds above are giggling loud,
While I search for wisdom in the crowd.

With every step, I trip and fall,
The map was written on a beach ball.
Birds are chirping, giving me hints,
But all I hear is my taste for mints.

Tides of Time and Treasure

Time's a tide that pulls and plays,
I checked my watch - it's lost its ways.
Searching for treasure in the sand,
I found a shoe, isn't life grand?

Seagulls squawk, they're in on the jest,
With maps that lead to another quest.
I tried to follow, but got distracted,
By a dancing crab, quite badly reacted.

The Quest for Hidden Clues

I seek for clues, with snacks in hand,
Just a cookie, helps me to stand.
Puzzles twist like pretzel knots,
As laughter rings from whimsical spots.

The treasure map had pizza stains,
Leading to fun instead of gains.
X marks the spot? I see a tree,
With a squirrel laughing, as it mocks me.

Navigating Through the Fog

Fog rolls in, thick and grey,
I squint hard, but lose my way.
Navigation skills are quite absurd,
When I'm convinced I heard a bird.

I fumble 'round with a paper guide,
It says go left, but I'm not that wide.
The signs are blurry, a cryptic mess,
Guess I'll just follow the fun, no stress!

Lighthouses in Tempestuous Waters

In stormy seas, we sail around,
With maps made of crumpled paper, found.
A seagull squawks, it gives me a wink,
"Don't rely on charts, just avoid the stink!"

With every wave, we navigate,
My compass spins, it's gone on a date.
The lighthouse beams, but what does it say?
"Y'all better steer clear, or drift away!"

Mapmakers of Memories and Dreams

We scribble our thoughts on the backs of napkins,
Crafting a journey of whenever we happening.
"Turn left at the cat," says my friend with flair,
But the cat just yawns, without a care.

On this treasure hunt, 'X' marks the smile,
But it's just a burrito, come back in a while.
With crayons and giggles, we sketch our way,
Though the paths get tangled, it's okay, hooray!

The Threads That Connect Us All

We're all just puppets with tangled strings,
Dancing in circles, can't find our wings.
"Thread lightly here," my buddy decrees,
But the knots keep tightening, oh, what a tease!

In this fabric of life, we crochet a laugh,
Stitching our mishaps, what a crazy craft.
"Pull on this thread!" one insists with glee,
Yet we unravel and trip, like a sighted bee!

The Odyssey of Unfulfilled Dreams

In a quest for grandeur, I packed up my hopes,
Rode a unicycle made of bubblegum ropes.
The map said 'GREAT,' but I ended up 'meh,'
Chasing squirrels who stole my sandwich, oh what a day!

Each step is a giggle, each turn is a jest,
Sailing in circles, I'm trying my best.
"Keep those dreams floaty!" my buddy declared,
But I keep crashing; my sea legs are impaired!

Every Step a Question

Why's the coffee always cold?
The toaster seems a bit too bold.
Each step I take, new thoughts arise,
Like where's my left shoe? Oh surprise!

Do I walk the dog or does he walk me?
Are we lost? Or is that just a spree?
The sidewalk's cracked, the map's all gone,
Yet here I am, still taggin' along!

Charting Stars in a Clouded Sky

I aimed for stars—found socks instead,
The constellation's under my bed!
Who knew the North Star's a fridge magnet?
And here's the Big Dipper—it's my regret!

With map in hand, I took a stroll,
Found a lost cat, claimed it my goal.
But the chart said to steer left, oh dear,
Now I'm three blocks down, still chasing a beer!

Footprints on Shifting Sands

Walked by the beach, shoes in my hand,
Who knew the tide would take my stand?
Each footprint fades, I keep on grinning,
In this game of hide-and-seek with winning!

Seagulls laugh as they swoop and dive,
They're the locals in this strange archive.
While I'm stuck wondering what's next on the way,
Maybe it's ice cream? That's my kind of play!

Echoes of Uncharted Destinies

I asked the mirror what's in store,
It only reflected my last cake score.
With echoes bouncing from wall to wall,
I'm still looking for my destiny ball!

Maps are confusing, did you hear?
Last week, I found treasure, oh dear!
But all it held was old cat hair,
And a compass that points to nowhere fair!

Splinters of Time and Space

In the attic of my brain, I found a shoe,
It had a tale to tell, who knew?
Time was stuck in the laces tight,
Jumbled maps in a cupboard of fright.

The clock kept ticking, or was it snoring?
It can't decide if it's lost or boring.
A cat sat there, pretending to read,
Whiskers twitching, fueling my need.

Suddenly, a squirrel joined the fray,
Mapping acorns in a very odd way.
Claiming this branch was once a great road,
A detour ahead; it's all just a code.

The faint smell of cookies wafts through the air,
The sweet scent of time, floating everywhere.
Splinters in the walls, stories to share,
Can I find my way, or do I just care?

The Seekers of the Trail Untamed

Two friends set out with a huge map,
Dressed in outfits that brightened the gap.
They tripped on roots; oh joy, how they danced,
Unraveled all paths, none was well-chanced.

They asked the trees for directions divine,
One pine just shrugged, 'I'm sipping wine.'
A rabbit hopped by, a guide? Who could tell?
Instead it just sneezed, 'Allergies, swell!'

With backpacks filled with dreams and some snacks,
They charged forth blindly, bringing on laughs.
A sign appeared that read 'Don't go that way!'
They smiled at danger, "Let's risk it today!"

In the end, they discovered no grand prize,
Just muddy boots and, oh, what a surprise!
While seeking the trail, they had fun instead,
Tracing laughter and joy in each word said.

Nature's Cartography of Experience

Trees point the way with their tangled arms,
Each leaf a whisper, each branch a charm.
A hedgehog rolls by, tiptoeing along,
With a map made of quills, what could go wrong?

The rivers giggle, tracing their lines,
Tickling the stones, composing sweet signs.
But the wind grows playful, pulls at my cap,
Stealing my compass, oh, what a mishap!

Clouds overhead like wandering sheep,
Wobbly and fluffy, they dance in a heap.
With each twist and turn, they lead me astray,
Perhaps I'll just float on the breeze for the day.

At the end of the trail, a fable unfolds,
Stories from nature, the best treasure told.
In search of a route, find joy in the game,
Who needs a map when the heart feels the same?

The Pilgrimage of the Inquisitive Heart

With a smartphone in hand, I'm seeking the way,
But the battery's low, what a terrible day!
I ask for directions from a dog on a stroll,
He cocks his head, I bet he knows the whole goal.

Across the park, a kid with a kite,
Sails upwards, drifting out of my sight.
"Which way to the fun?" I call with glee,
He shouts back a riddle, "Only you can see!"

Through bushes and trails, my feet start to roam,
With laughter as footsteps, I'm far from home.
Every turn brings a smile, or perhaps some dread,
But what's not known is better than what's read.

In the twilight glow, with friends all around,
We create our map, in laughter we're bound.
A pilgrimage of hearts, so curious and bright,
Knowing every wrong turn is just part of the flight.

The Art of Finding The Unfindable

I searched for answers near the chair,
But all I found was old cat hair.
With socks mismatched, I stroll along,
Where did I leave my keys? Oh, wrong!

I ventured up a winding stair,
Found my lunch that I forgot there.
A map would've helped my weary quest,
But instead, I just took a rest.

The fridge, it hums a lullaby,
As I ponder where the lost socks lie.
Not all who wander are truly lost,
But it seems I'm collecting chaos at cost!

A compass, a guide, or maybe some snacks,
These are the tools for my crazy tracks.
Mapping my days with giggles and sighs,
Life's puzzle pieces, a jumbled surprise!

A Journey Through the Labyrinth of Being

I bought a book on how to be wise,
But it turned out just to be a surprise.
With pages torn and some food stains,
I questioned my sanity and its remains.

A winding path through my own mind,
Where logic is lost, yet somehow I find,
The shoe on the left and the right shoe, too,
Both missing the point, but what else is new?

I stumbled into a clever debate,
With squirrels that claim they control fate.
"Nutty ambitions! Join us," they said,
So I followed their trail, trusting my head.

Through twists and turns, I laughed all the way,
Reality's map? I tossed it away.
Embracing the chaos, I twirled and spun,
In this unplanned journey, I'm still having fun!

Intersections of Fate and Dreams

At the corner of hopes and wild schemes,
I met a chicken hitching her dreams.
She crossed the road with a questionable wink,
To find a lost key? Or just a good drink?

I stumbled upon a fork in the lane,
One path led to pillows, the other to grain.
Algorithms claim I should take the first,
But I'm too busy chasing my hiccuping thirst.

Beneath the streetlight, a shadow did sway,
A whimsical dance at the end of the day.
With life's intersections, I cracked a big smile,
Embracing the silly, one glorious mile.

I found the directions were lost in a tweet,
But who needs a map when laughter's so sweet?
In the chaos of roads, I twinkled and gleamed,
Life's crazy ballet is more fun than it seemed!

The Intrigue of Unraveled Threads

In a pile of yarn, I found my muse,
With tangled threads and some old shoes.
I tried to knit the fabric of fate,
But instead, it just knitted my own great wait.

Each stitch unraveled to reveal a tale,
Of missed opportunities and a flat tire's wail.
I fumbled with needles, made a nice mess,
But in that chaos, found sweet happiness.

With colors bright and patterns absurd,
I stitched a story without any word.
Who needs a guide when you've got a hook?
I transformed confusion into my own book.

In the tapestry of wild dreams, I weave,
Finding beauty in the threads I believe.
So here's to the messy, the strange, and the fun,
In this wacky adventure, I'm never done!

Parables of the Journey Without Destination

A duck with a suitcase, quite bold and spry,
Waddling through fields with a gleam in its eye.
The map in its beak? It was just a receipt,
Not quite the treasure, yet still quite the feat.

Chickens on bicycles, racing the breeze,
Squawking about fun, and doing it with ease.
They've lost their direction, but oh, what a race,
With no finish line, they just laugh and embrace.

Frames of Reference in Uncertain Times

A turtle in glasses, reading the guide,
Said, "Keep your pace slow, it's lonely outside!"
The rabbit nearby just chuckled with glee,
"Maps aren't for me, I'm too fast, can't you see?"

The squirrel took selfies, it captured the day,
While pondering life in a whimsical way.
It posted, then laughed, "Hashtag wander with style!"
For deeper reflections, it's just not my trial.

The Hunt for Hidden Clues

A fox in a trench coat, looking so sly,
Searching for clues 'neath the bright, sunny sky.
Found a sock and a pebble, declared it a win,
"Perhaps life is puzzles, let's see what's within!"

An owl perched high, croaking, "What's the plan?"
"I can't find my map, can you lend me a hand?"
With a wink, the fox said, "Just follow your nose!"
Sometimes the best clues are the ones that we chose!

Echoes of the Road Less Traveled

There once was a snail on a trail made of thyme,
Singing to flowers, taking it one rhyme at a time.
"Step where you want, there's no hurry in store!"
As it sipped on some dew, it winked at the floor.

Two ants in a car, playing tunes from the past,
"Take a left at the grapevine, let's drive really fast!"
But alas, they hit traffic—a web made of leaves,
Yet in laughter and chaos, they found sweet reprieves.

The Map of Wishes and Dreams

I drew a map with crayons, red,
A treasure chest beneath my bed.
With arrows pointing left and right,
But where's the X? It's out of sight.

The compass spins, it makes me laugh,
I think it wants a bubble bath.
With each wrong turn, I trip and fall,
But giggle through it, after all.

A pirate's life is full of glee,
But where's my ship? Oh, woe is me!
I'll sail the seas with snacks and dreams,
And maybe find those golden beams.

The map I made, it leads to snack,
Hot fudge sundaes, a tasty track.
So here's my quest, a joyful spree,
Mapping dessert, just you and me!

Carving Paths in the Wilderness of Thought

In forests deep where thoughts may roam,
I carved a path to call my home.
With sticks and stones, and lots of twine,
I lost my way, but isn't that fine?

I took a turn where squirrels chatter,
Wondering why my shoes don't flatter.
A hedgehog stopped to share some tea,
And said, "Just follow me, you see!"

We doodled maps made of sweet cream,
Exploring the land of the absurd dream.
Each twist and turn a giggly game,
With every wrong step, just more fame!

So here I wander, lost and free,
Earning badges from the trees.
In this wild place where thoughts entwine,
I carve my path, it's all divine!

Beyond the Veil of Everyday

Past morning coffee and rush hour grind,
Lies a world where dreams unwind.
With socks mismatched and hair a mess,
Adventure waits in each new dress.

I peek behind the fridge one day,
Hoping to find a lost ballet.
Instead, I found a sock brigade,
Planning a dance in the hallway shade.

The garden gnomes plot to escape,
While laundry piles take on new shape.
With every mundane task I do,
I find the magic hiding too.

So here's to daily life's delight,
Where silly antics bring us light.
Beyond the bland, the strange unfold,
In every corner, laughter's gold!

The Language of Unfinished Sentences

I left my thoughts half-baked and sweet,
Like cookies lingering in the heat.
A word here lost, a phrase misplaced,
But in the gaps, new jokes are graced.

While pondering why socks disappear,
I scribble nonsense, laughter near.
"A giraffe once danced with a broom,"
My brain's a cluttered, joyful room.

The cat just laughed at my attempts,
To finish lines that made no sense.
But every thought's a chance to jest,
In scrambled words, we find our best!

So here's to chats that go awry,
To silly tales we cannot try.
In unfinished words, we craft our cheer,
A language filled with joy and beer!

The Quest Beyond the Horizon

In search of treasure, I drew a map,
Only to find it led to a nap.
X marks the spot where I lost my shoe,
Maybe I'll find the meaning in stew.

My compass points right, but I turn left,
Seems I'm more adrift than I thought I bereft.
Each step I take leads to a new snack,
But answers are hidden behind a snack pack.

With every wrong turn, I chuckle and grin,
Is it gold I seek, or just leftover din?
The horizon calls with a laugh and a tease,
Perhaps the maps just want me to freeze!

So here I stand, with my face in a pie,
If this is the quest, oh why oh why?
Adventure awaits with a grin that's so broad,
Maybe the map's just an elaborate facade.

Labyrinths of the Heart

Inside my chest beats a curious heart,
It has a tendency to wander and dart.
One day it's joy, the next it's dismay,
A maze made of feelings that twist and sway.

I mapped out my feelings with crayons and glue,
But each emotion just seems to skew.
Love's a roundabout that never quite ends,
And friendship's a treadmill with misplaced bends.

Why does sweet laughter come with some tears?
Maybe life's manual forgot to include gears.
I searched for a guide in a box made of wine,
To find that the answers are mostly just fine.

But through all the chaos, I giggle aloud,
With friends by my side, I'm already blessed and proud.
In the labyrinth I dance, taking turns with some flair,
'Cause really, who needs a map if you care?

Shadows of a Wandering Spirit

My spirit wanders like a lost little child,
Taking detours, oh so wild.
It thinks it's smart with its winks and its sighs,
But trips on its shoelace, oh what a surprise!

The shadows loom large when I try to be sly,
I dodge and I dart like a butterfly spry.
"Where's my direction?" I shout to the sky,
It replies with echoes and a ten-foot spy.

I take a wrong turn at a burger stand,
Now I'm a connoisseur of ketchup on hand.
Each step feels silly, but do I care to fret?
Every strange path makes a memory I won't regret.

Eventually I'll find my place in the night,
But for now, I'll dance; everything feels just right.
With shadows as partners, I'll lead the parade,
For wandering's charm is a game to be played.

The Unwritten Road Ahead

An empty road stretches, no signs in sight,
I take out my snacks, it's a delightful bite.
My future's unwritten, like a blank page,
Yet I scribble some doodles, it starts to engage.

Each pothole I hit makes me giggle and sway,
These bumps in the road just want me to play.
With every mile marker, I wave and I cheer,
"Keep it coming, Universe, I'm ready, my dear!"

The maps say I'm lost, but I think I'm found,
In this jazzy jam session, life's so profound.
The unwritten scroll has the best twists and bends,
Where laughter and joy are my ultimate friends.

So onward I drive with no schedule to keep,
With dreams in the rearview, I giggle and leap.
The road ahead sparkles, a shimmering thread,
In the adventure of now, I've got nothing to dread.

Navigating the Unknown

With a map that's upside down,
I'm wandering through this town.
Birds might sing but I'll be,
As lost as lost can be.

The GPS says turn right,
But somehow I face the night.
Follow the yellow brick road?
Wait, is that my neighbor's abode?

I stopped to ask a friendly face,
"Excuse me, where's my special place?"
He pointed to a giant tree,
And said, "That's where you should be!"

So I dance beneath the stars,
With nothing but my dreams and scars.
I'll map it out, I must insist,
But first, I need to find my list!

The Compass of Dreams

A compass that spins just for fun,
Is not a tool for the good run.
I follow where the needle tips,
And end up with embarrassing slips.

Each dream I chase takes me askew,
Left or right? I've no clue!
Is that my goal or a pizza shop?
I guess I'll stop and take a mop.

Wind blows and I'm tossed around,
Finding treasure under the ground.
Is that a diamond? Or just some gum?
While dreaming of the riches to come!

So I giggle through the twists and turns,
For every lesson, my heart still burns.
With my quirky compass map in hand,
I navigate this whimsical land!

In Search of Forgotten Paths

I seek a trail that's lost in time,
But every step feels like a rhyme.
"Is it here?" I scratch my head,
Or was it in that book I read?

The trees whisper secrets from the past,
I laugh aloud, "Will it last?"
Dancing leaves and shadows leap,
While I pretend to take a peep.

A squirrel scurries, claims the lead,
"Follow me!" That's all I need.
But I trip over roots galore,
And fall down to explore the floor.

In the chaos, I find some fun,
The path is there, just not the one!
So here I stand, a map in my mind,
In search of paths that are hard to find!

Unfolding the Unseen Journey

I packed my bags with snacks and glee,
Ready for a grand journey.
A map unfolds with goofy lines,
While my coffee spills through the signs.

The road ahead, twists like a snake,
I'm wondering if it's real or fake.
"Turn left!" shouts my friend so bold,
But we really need to find the gold!

Every turn reveals surprise and cheer,
Who knew the circus would also steer?
With juggling clowns and pies galore,
I can't help but laugh and explore.

So here's the trick to journeys unseen,
Join the madness, it's quite routine.
With every step, I find a grin,
In this wild world, let the fun begin!

The Riddle of Lost Roads

I packed my bags for a trip so grand,
With snacks and maps all perfectly planned.
But where's the train and where's the plane?
I think I took a wrong turn again.

The GPS says I'm on a path so true,
Yet here I am, stuck in a zoo.
The lions laugh as I look around,
I swear my exit was just here, bound.

My compass spins, my sandwich is lost,
Turns out my journey has a hefty cost.
Each twist and turn is just a big joke,
Am I driving or playing some kind of poke?

So here's my advice to all who roam,
When lost in the wild, just call it home.
Embrace the chaos, it's all in good fun,
When maps seem silly, then let's just run!

Unraveling the Threads of Existence

I pondered my purpose under a flickering light,
As socks lost their pairs and I lost my sight.
I stared at the chaos of my attic space,
Is this where wisdom hides, or just a rat race?

I tried to decipher the mess I made,
Why are cereal boxes stacked like a barricade?
Between the crumbs and the empty cups,
Is my future waiting or just giving up?

I searched for signs in my pile of clothes,
Where did I hang my ambitions, who knows?
A sassy shirt says, "Just chill and reset,"
Perhaps it's telling me, "Don't lose your bet!"

So here I stand, a thread in the loom,
Laughing at life as it spins in my room.
When questions pile up, don't take it to heart,
Sometimes the fabric needs a little good art!

The Journey We Never Mark

I walked a path that led to a bean,
My travel journal? Just a can of green.
Each step I took felt oddly misplaced,
Were my shoes trailing mud or just a funny taste?

With each twist and turn, the road seemed new,
I met a goat who whispered, 'What's wrong with you?'
I asked for directions, she chewed some hay,
"Just follow your nose," she wisely did say.

I circled around, a dance with a lamp,
Was my goal to discover or just find a stamp?
The journey unfolds with laughter and cheer,
Who knew wandering could lead to good beer?

So mark not your journey with X's and O's,
But with silly tales and the joy it bestows.
For in every wrong turn, a lesson awaits,
Keep dancing with goats, for life's full of fates!

A Canvas of Questions

I grabbed a brush, a canvas so bright,
To paint my thoughts on a whimsical night.
But every stroke turned into a quirk,
Wait, is that a giraffe or just my work?

I mixed theories with whimsy and fun,
Created a scene of a three-legged run.
"What does it mean?" asked a curious crow,
I shrugged and said, "It's all for the show!"

My colors splashed with a brush of glee,
A masterpiece born from sheer folly.
Each question I threw became part of the mix,
Is freedom a dog in a yoga fix?

So here's my reply to the canvas I scrawl,
Just laugh at the questions and let your heart haul.
For art has no answers, just giggles and cheer,
In the gallery of life, my friends, run here!

Footfalls Upon Untrodden Soil

With each step that I take, I wonder,
Is this path a gift or just a blunder?
The ground beneath is soft and squishy,
Like my hopes and dreams, a little mushy.

I stumble on stones that giggle and tease,
Each misstep begs, 'Aren't you pleased?'
I dance with the grass, as it sways and sighs,
As puzzled ants march in straight little lines.

A map would help, I think I'd agree,
But maybe I should just follow the bee.
With its buzzing wisdom and flitting cheer,
I'll embrace the chaos and swallow my fear.

Footfalls echo on untrodden grounds,
Where laughter and whims intertwine and rebound.
I'll skip and I'll hop, and with joy I'll proclaim,
In this wildest of searches, I'm winning the game!

Constellations of Choices

My head is a sky, a mix of bright stars,
Some shine like wisdom, others have scars.
I wish for a telescope, perhaps a guide,
To chart out decisions I hide in my stride.

If only I knew which way to glance,
This cosmic dance feels more like a trance.
A fork in the road, oh what a delight,
Should I wear the purple or stick with white?

Each choice is a planet, spinning around,
With gravity pulling, I'm oft' spellbound.
Should I venture forth or just stay in bed?
Maybe choose dinner from the food truck instead?

So here I sit, with stars on my mind,
In the universe of choices, I've fallen behind.
I'll scribble my wishes upon dark slate,
And hope the cosmos will pick up my fate!

The Paradox of Direction

I've got a compass, but it spins in loops,
Leading me straight into gatherings of poops.
The north is a puzzle and south is a jest,
I'm more lost than found in this wild quest.

The signs by the road are like riddles unsolved,
I'm winding around while all problems evolve.
An arrow points left; I'm drawn to the right,
Is this life's great joke or just moonlight?

A treasure map? Oh dear, what a bore,
I prefer the spur-of-the-moment explore.
With every choice marked with laughter and joy,
I guess I'll keep plodding, like a lost little boy.

Direction, sweet paradox, keeping me grinning,
In circles I wander but oh, isn't it spinning?
With every wrong turn, I might just be right,
For out of the chaos, stars twinkle bright!

In the Silence of Unanswered Queries

Questions, oh questions, they tickle my brain,
Like squirrels in a race, there's no need for the pain.
I crave the cliff notes, the shortcuts to truth,
But wander alone, chasing echoes of youth.

In silence, I ponder, I shrug and I sigh,
An uncharted ocean, I float, oh so high.
Why do the socks always disappear?
Is there an answer, or am I just queer?

I seek and I search, for wisdom untold,
In the stillness, I chuckle, as mysteries unfold.
An astronaut's journey on a paper boat,
In this wild journey, it's laughter I tote.

In silence, sweet queries keep me awake,
I play with the questions, dance on the lake.
With each splash of confusion, I'm still floating free,
In the silence of wonders, oh how fun to be me!

Vagabonds in Search of Meaning

We wandered far, lost in thought,
With only a map that we bought.
It showed a path, somewhat unclear,
And led us to a land of beer.

We danced with squirrels, sang with crows,
Debated if we were real pros.
Our compass spun, our laughs took flight,
In search of answers through the night.

A wise old tree said with a grin,
"Perhaps the fun's where you begin!"
We scratched our heads and chewed on gum,
While pondering what truly was fun.

With every twist, our questions grew,
Like chasing shadows in the blue.
Yet in our hearts, a spark would gleam,
A joke or two, the heart's own theme.

The River Between What Is and What Could Be

I paddled hard in my tiny boat,
Crossing a river filled with quote.
Each line I read, a silly jest,
Left me unsure what's best for the quest.

The current pulled, my oars went whack,
A rubber duck chased my snack.
What is this place? A riddle spun,
A riverbank where giggles run.

On either side, the grass was green,
But both the shores seemed quite obscene.
I shouted loud, "Is this the way?"
A frog exclaimed, "Just seize the day!"

With paddle high, I made a splash,
Floating dreams in a happy dash.
The river laughed with every wave,
A funny dance, a quest so brave.

A Journey Through the Canvas of Time

With brush in hand, I painted fate,
Each stroke a giggle, not a weight.
Time dripped down like melting cheese,
Creating scenes that made us wheeze.

Whimsical clouds, a smiling sun,
Birds in bow ties, oh what fun!
We tripped on colors, danced on lines,
Chasing answers mixed with wines.

Each corner turned brought laughs anew,
A portrait here, a pirate crew.
The canvas whispered jokes so sly,
"Who needs a map? Just try, oh my!"

In vivid hues, our dreams still linger,
As we paint joy with each finger.
With every sip, the night grew bright,
In this wild art, we found our light.

Echoes of Aspirations Yet To Be

In a forest deep with echoes loud,
We stumbled through a thinking crowd.
Each whispered wish danced by our side,
A parade of hopes we could not hide.

With every step, we cracked a smile,
As trees debated in their style.
One claimed truths, another jest,
While we just giggled as our quest.

The path ahead was filled with fog,
Where dreams and laughter chased a dog.
He barked the tunes of plans undone,
Turning our thoughts into pure fun.

So, onward we wandered, hearts so free,
Through echoes of what we could be.
Our aspirations, silly and bright,
Brought us together, pure delight.

Wandering Gazes Towards Distant Horizons

Eyes fixed wide on the skyline's grins,
Searching for wisdom in stray cat spins.
Map corners curled like grandma's old quilt,
A compass that insists on spinning at will.

Cup of coffee, two sugars, or maybe three,
Chasing the taste of perplexity.
Each step a question, each laugh a clue,
The sky, a stage for our wild preview.

A Quest for Threads of Meaning

In a world where socks disappear at will,
I ponder profound thoughts with a pillow's thrill.
Chasing down quests in a pair of flip-flops,
While hunting for wisdom in cereal shops.

They say the journey's half the fun, oh dear!
So I stop to tickle the nearest reindeer.
Pondering puzzles with every small breath,
Or deciphering laughter 'til there's none left.

Theories of Why We Roam

Why do we wander and chuckle so bright?
Is it the snacks, or is it just right?
With mismatched shoes and a smile so wide,
Every wrong turn brings joy as a guide.

Maps are for people with shoes tied tight,
I prefer to skip, dance, and take flight.
Philosophers mumble, trying to think deep,
But I find more wisdom in the cat's sleepy heap.

Signposts Built on Thoughts

Signposts made of candy canes and dreams,
Guide me to places that make my heart beam.
With thought bubbles floating like balloons in the sky,
Each giggle a beacon as time slips by.

I scribble my plans on a napkin of hope,
While wondering if my barista can soap.
Using wishes as fuel for this silly race,
With each blunder I make, I just quicken my pace.

The Cartographer's Dream

In a world of maps that don't exist,
I scribble paths that twist and twist.
The North is down, the South is right,
And every star is a failed flight.

With crayons bright, I shade the seas,
Add islands made of Swiss cheese.
A road that leads to nowhere fast,
A style that's bold, but no contrast.

I search for routes in every snack,
The only guide is a hungry knack.
Hey, that's a treasure! Or so I dream,
A golden nugget or a soft ice cream.

So here I sit with crayons spent,
No GPS, but pure intent.
In every mess lies true delight,
I'm the lost king, but that's all right.

Stars that Light the Darkened Way

Beneath the sky, I scan for signs,
But all I find are pizza lines.
A star is lost, a comet's called,
The universe has been installed.

With each twinkle, I dare to guess,
Is that a goal or just a mess?
I'll catch the stardust on my face,
And hope it leads to a better place.

Yet here I wait, a cosmic fool,
Using stars as my GPS tool.
Finding fate in a pizza pie,
If only wishes weren't a lie!

So look above when you feel blue,
Maybe a star's just waiting for you.
A world of chaos can gleam and sway,
On this funny, starry stage we play.

Shadows of Purpose in a Wandering World

In shadows deep, I wander wide,
With laughter echoing as my guide.
What shadowed path leads to the prize?
Or just more pizza with funny fries?

Each step I take, I trip and fall,
Pick myself up, laugh through it all.
A shadow whispers, 'Turn around!',
Only to find I'm pizza-bound.

With purpose unclear and humor bright,
I dance with shadows in the night.
A waltz with doubt, a jig with glee,
My map's a joke, but that's okay with me.

So in this world where shadows prance,
I'll keep on dancing, take a chance.
In every stumble, joy unfurls,
Finding purpose in these quirky whirls.

Seeking Signposts in the Fog

Through furry fog, I wander blind,
With every twist, surprises bind.
A signpost here directs me wrong,
But oh, what fun to skip along!

I squint and search for words of gold,
But it's just soup that's gone too cold.
"Left or right?" I shout aloud,
The fog just giggles, proud and loud.

Each moment's lost, a merry game,
In the thick mist, I lost my name.
A compass spins, a guide's on break,
But laughter rises with each mistake.

So let the fog wrap me in fun,
For in this haze, we all are one.
With every stumble, my spirit jives,
In this silly dance, my heart survives.

Threads of Destiny Interwoven

In a tapestry, I roam each thread,
Finding knots where I fear to tread.
I've tied my shoes, but lost my way,
Chasing dreams like kids with clay.

A map in crayon, bright and bold,
Points to treasures, yet untold.
But GPS says, 'you're on your way,'
To a coffee shop, two blocks away.

The more I search, the less I find,
In cereal boxes, clues unwind.
The cat looks wise with a tilted head,
As if she knows where I'll be led.

Life's a game of hide and seek,
With each new turn, a chance to peek.
I shrug my shoulders, laugh and grin,
In this maze, we all might win.

The Untold Stories of Every Footstep

Each step I take, a story missed,
Like socks lost in a laundry twist.
I wander paths of rubber trees,
With shoe prints left to tease the breeze.

A duck quacks loud, gives me advice,
Says, 'Don't fret, just roll the dice!'
My feet sometimes take a wild leap,
While I just wish for shoes that beep.

With every mile, an awkward dance,
Tripping over life's odd romance.
I wave to ants, they wave back too,
And life becomes a funny zoo.

At every corner, fortune smiles,
Sometimes silly, but always worthwhile.
With missteps marked in chalk so bright,
I trace my path, a laugh in sight.

Whispers of Tomorrow in Today's Embrace

Tomorrow whispers in my ear,
'Stop and smell some chocolate cheer!'
While calendar pages flip like birds,
My plans dissolve into cheerful words.

Each hour ticks by with playful glee,
Chasing shadows that run from me.
I chase my dreams on a unicycle,
Laughter echoes like a light cycle.

The sandwich I dropped finds a new friend,
A wayward crumb, a twist to blend.
With each mishap, I trip and sway,
'What's next?' I ask, as time holds sway.

A fortune cookie cracks with zest,
'Take it slow and find your quest.'
I smile, embrace the fate I see,
Tomorrow's whispers laugh with me.

Charting the Course of Uncertainty

I set my sails on winds so light,
With directions scribbled in past night's fright.
The stars all laugh from up above,
While I'm lost in a sea of love.

A compass spins, it can't decide,
Which way to go, so I just glide.
Maps are useless, they twist and bend,
Like jokes that loop without an end.

The waves keep pushing, a gentle shove,
As I navigate with a rubber glove.
The seagulls giggle, they plan to mock,
As I steer my ship without a dock.

But in the chaos, joy sets sail,
Life's a ride, not just a trail.
So here I float with tea in hand,
Charting fun where what's unplanned.

The Inkling of a Guiding Light

In a world of twists and turns,
I found a sock, but where's the fern?
I asked a turtle for his take,
He just smiled and offered cake.

A compass spins, a phone's in hand,
Alexa says, "Just take a stand."
But standing still just makes me crave,
A map to find the snack bar wave.

Maps Made of Memories

My childhood map is full of fries,
I scribbled roads 'neath ketchup skies.
With every bite, a journey starts,
To lands where candy fills our carts.

The crayon paths are faded now,
But gummy bears still take a bow.
I'll draw new routes with chocolate pens,
And wander back to those sweet ends.

Searching for the North Star

A nightlight glows, my guiding star,
It shines while I've misplaced my car.
I searched the driveway, then the street,
Turns out I parked by the dog's seat.

Constellations made of pizza slices,
In space, not all are good advice.
I'll navigate with cheesy glee,
And maybe find my car by tea.

Over Mountains and Through Valleys

Through mountains steep, my breath is caught,
I tripped on rocks, forgot the thought.
My hiking boots are quite the mess,
But hey, at least I've got my dress!

The valley calls with echoes loud,
I yell back, feeling rather proud.
But nature's map is a bit blurred,
I'll ask the squirrel; he'd say a word.

Wandering Without a Destination

Lost in a maze, I stroll with glee,
Map upside down, like me a little cheesy.
Where's the next stop, oh where could it be?
A squirrel just waved, is he guiding me free?

I asked a cactus for directions quite bold,
He just stood there, pointy and cold.
With a smile, I shrugged, bright as a gold,
Guess I'll wander till I'm finally sold!

In circles I go, my feet start to tire,
But wait, look! A donut shop's on the flyer!
A snack is a map, can't say I'm a liar,
With coffee in hand, my heart's on fire.

So here I will sit, laughing at fate,
With sprinkles and cream, just drinking this plate.
Wandering's fun, I'll simply create,
A path made of pastries, life's sweetest state.

Treading Lightly on the Trail

Tiptoe through weeds, I dance with delight,
A butterfly flutters, how nice is the sight?
Beneath the green leaves, I'm taking my flight,
Tripped on a twig, but hey, it's alright!

The squirrels are plotting, I swear I can see,
In a meeting or secret, just look at them flee!
They hide all the nuts, like it's just for me,
I'll barter a snack, how funny they be!

With each step I take, my shoes squeak a tune,
Like a whimsical witch in bright afternoon.
Galloping forth, I'll charm every moon,
Until someone stops me and says, "What a loon!"

The trees start to giggle, I can hear the sounds,
The grass plays a jingle, while spinning around.
Nature's my buddy, no need for crowns,
Just a hop and a skip, life's joy abounds.

The Quest for Unseen Paths

Onward I march, where to, I just don't know,
A treasure map sketched on the back of a crow.
With breadcrumbs and giggles, I'm putting on a show,
Searching for meaning in the streams that flow.

Shiny rocks twinkle, "Pick me!" they say,
But trip on a stone, now my shoes are at bay.
What's under this bush? A fortune or hay?
A gnome with a cactus? I'll ask him to play!

Through valleys and hills, my compass spins round,
It points to the place where oddities abound.
A frog in a tux, how splendidly crowned,
He croaks 'You're a fool but you dance to the sound!'

So on this grand quest, I'll don my best hat,
With mismatched socks, I'm an odd little brat.
Finding the joy in each step, how bout that?
With friends made of whimsy, I'm always where's at!

Navigating the Unknown Seas

Loosely I float on this floppy old boat,
With maps made of jelly, that wiggle and gloat.
The fish laugh and swim, 'Are you 'lost'? Take a note!
My compass is broken, I'm just a fun quote!

The sky's doing pirouettes, clouds all around,
A seagull keeps squawking like he owns the sound.
With waves like a dance floor, it's trouble I've found,
But who needs a plan when the laughter is bound?

My anchor's a sandwich, it holds me in place,
As jellyfish float by in a gooey embrace.
Sailing this sea, it's a topsy-turvy grace,
With laughter as wind, the horizon I chase.

So here on these waters, I gleefully glide,
With a map made of crayons, I'll take on the tide.
Adventures await, in this boat, I'll abide,
Mapping joy with each wave, my heart open wide.

Unraveled Roads and Hidden Signs

I took a wrong turn at the clock,
A GPS that only knows to mock.
Those detours led to ice cream wheels,
And laughter is how the heart feels.

Maps crumpled in the backseat's fold,
With every twist, new tales unfold.
A sign for 'lost' in neon bright,
I'm steering left into the night.

Bumps and pits hide secrets well,
Like fortune cookies with tales to tell.
From crossroads of coffee to bumpers of fun,
Who knew the journey could weigh a ton?

So on I roll with snacks in tow,
Each wrong turn is a brand new show.
With giggles echoing through my ride,
Who needs a map with joy as my guide?

The Algorithm of Existence

They say there's a code, a secret key,
But I'm stuck at 'Hello' by my cup of tea.
Every formula's just a joke undone,
Like calculating how much fun I've spun.

Variables dance like they're in a trance,
While constants stare, forgetting the prance.
Graphs ZOOM in and out like they're on a spree,
Trying to find out who the heck is me.

I've coded my breakfast; it's much too bright,
The toast just winked - is that alright?
De-bugging life just feels so absurd,
Algorithms can't catch a single word.

So give me the chaos, the pure heart's song,
No algorithms here - just all night long.
With laughter mixed in the chaos of fate,
Let the universe jest; it's a wild date!

Mist on the Horizon of Discovery

The sunrise giggles, shrouded in grey,
Whispers of secrets that wander astray.
I open my map, blank as my mind,
Hoping for treasures, but find I'm confined.

Thick fog cloaks the answers I seek,
Like a cat burglar that never speaks.
I stumble upon a wild goose chase,
In a world where directions go at their own pace.

A compass spins like it's lost in a spin,
Finding north through the wild cat's din.
With each twist and turn, I chase the cloud,
Stumbling onward, oh, so proud!

Yet, in the haze, I find a delight,
That getting lost makes the laughter ignite.
For every foggy turn that I roam,
Leads to peculiar tales I gladly call home.

Questions that Dance Amongst the Stars

Questions twirl like stars in the night,
With glow-in-the-dark shoes that feel just right.
Do aliens have tea, or just fancy brew?
And if so, what's their favorite stew?

Do clouds giggle when it rains so?
Do sunbeams dare to dance in a row?
While shooting stars whisper quirky rhymes,
I'm jotting them down for future times.

Are asteroids bored, drifting in space?
Or just practicing for a cosmic race?
In this celestial party, I feel out of place,
But I'll twirl and spin with a warm embrace.

So I'll ponder those whims while munching on cheese,
Counting my wishes with the greatest of ease.
For the universe spins a delightful jest,
And in this vast void, I feel truly blessed!

Pathways of Curiosity and Wonder

In a world of twists and bends,
We wander with our goofy friends,
Seeking clues under odd-shaped rocks,
While dodging squirrels in their funny frocks.

Each step we take feels like a game,
With laughter, joy, and not much fame,
We giggle at our silly maps,
Picturing treasure, perhaps some naps.

Through forests thick and valleys wide,
We trip and slip, but we take it in stride,
For every stumble leads to a smile,
Adventure awaits, let's stay awhile!

So bring your quirks and wild intent,
For the best of paths are often bent,
With every wrong turn, we find delight,
In this silly quest, from day to night.

A Treasure Map Yet to be Drawn

A map of x's is hard to find,
Especially when you're this unkind,
With arrows pointing every which way,
Where's the treasure? Who's got the say?

In cardboard castles, we craft our fate,
Drawing paths on plates, can you relate?
Our compass spins like a wild dance,
Oh, where's the gold? We forgot to glance!

With each new wrinkle, the plot thickens,
Laughter erupts as confusion quickens,
Maybe the treasure is just a snack,
A cookie to share before we look back.

With laughter echoing, we take a seat,
And ponder if this map is sweet,
The journey continues, let's pace our lore,
With humor as currency, we always want more!

The Dance of Questions and Uncertainty

Twirl and swirl, what's your next quest?
Is it north, south, or perhaps a jest?
Questions flutter like butterflies bold,
With answers hiding, or so we're told.

Dare we ask, 'Is this the right track?'
While the map bobbles, we check for a snack,
Each puzzle piece is a laugh waiting,
In the dance of doubt, we're celebrating.

With every riddle, let's turn it around,
Maybe a jest is where joy is found,
We leap on one foot, we wiggle our toes,
In this funny waltz, anything goes!

Through questions that bounce like a rubber ball,
We chase the answers, always enthralled,
With giggles and quirks, we carry on,
Turning uncertainty into a funny song!

Luminescence in the Darkness of Doubt

In shadows deep where the critters creep,
We search for flickers, our laughter to keep,
With lanterns made of marshmallows bright,
We stumble around in the soft moonlight.

"What if this path leads us astray?"
"Just make it a joke! We'll be fine anyway!"
With each little bump, our chuckles collide,
In the glow of our giggles, we take it in stride.

Worries dissolve like sugar in tea,
With every mishap, we're simply carefree,
A game of hide and seek with our doubt,
Who knew uncertainty could make us shout?

So here's to the journey, both silly and real,
With laughter like sunshine, our hearts we will heal,
Through darkness and humor, together we'll roam,
For in every twist, we are finally home!

Roads Less Taken

I took a turn where the signs were vague,
Found a path marked in coffee stains,
Silly me, chasing dreams like a hag,
Now I'm lost in my own terrain.

GPS? Nah, that thing likes to tease,
Says 'recalculating' like it's big fun,
I'm waving at gardens as I squeeze,
Chasing clouds under the clueless sun.

I've met a tree that claimed to talk,
But all it said was 'leaf me alone',
Maybe the stump will teach me to walk,
I promise I won't whine or groan.

If life's a trip filled with silly charm,
Then hand me a map with glitter and spark,
I'll strut through chaos, no need for alarm,
On this merry no-path, let's embark!

The Elusive Signposts

Oh, the signs are quirky, like they know a joke,
'Next left at the purple goat,' they claim,
I laugh so hard, nearly 'til I choke,
As I dance down this whimsical lane.

Every twist is strange, like spaghetti al dente,
Here's hoping the compass has a sense of humor,
Its needle spins like it's at a frenzy,
While I'm left pondering why I'm a bloomer.

Got a map folded, looks more like origami,
Twists and turns all lead to nowhere,
I'm the punchline of my own comedy,
Staring at clouds, pretending they're air.

For every wrong turn, there's laughter to gain,
With each detour, I'll ride on the silly,
This journey's absurd, yet that's my domain,
Wandering free, oh so very frilly!

Beneath the Surface of Wanderlust

Wanderlust wears mismatched socks,
Sprinting toward the moon with glee,
Roads look like scribbles in kids' blocks,
And yet, they lead me where I need to be.

Beneath this zest, I hear my heart giggle,
'Caution: explore; don't be a bore,'
Each stumbling step is just a wiggle,
Shuffling through doors for some absurd lore.

I fumble with paths like a jester's hat,
Every misstep is a merry blunder,
Wear my silliness; it's where I'm at,
Chasing shadows, creating my wonder.

In the chaos of aimless whimsied dreams,
There's joy in the dance of a freckled fate,
With laughter woven through life's little seams,
I'll wink at the stars as I close the gate.

Paths in the Garden of Chance

In the garden, paths twist like pretzels,
Each turn brings giggles, what a sight,
Was that a sign or just my mental vessels?
Turning left at the gnome, feels just right.

The flowers nod like they know my plight,
'Here's your map,' they seem to say,
But all I can do is laugh, hold on tight,
As my umbrella flips in the blustery sway.

Butterflies tease with their flutter and flit,
Leading me circles like I'm in a spin,
At every corner, life throws a hit,
Yet I'm still grinning, let the fun begin!

If chance is the gardener, I'll prune with glee,
Tending the rows of my nonsensical path,
With a trowel of whimsy, just me and me,
Let's plant the seeds of an unexpected laugh!

The Puzzle of a Thousand Pieces

In a box, I found a scene,
Scattered bits, oh where's the queen?
I search for edges, all just gray,
Where'd I put my snacks today?

A corner piece rolls under the chair,
I swear it was just standing there!
Each time I fit a piece in place,
My cat jumps in, it's a race!

The picture's vague, it's like a joke,
Did I drop it, or just choke?
It says 'fun', but is it real?
Or just a game to make me squeal?

With each mistake I heave a sigh,
Where's the fumbling map? I cry!
Yet as I laugh at this great plight,
I say it's fun – at least tonight!

Fleeting Moments

A tick-tock clock with hands that race,
I missed my ride, oh what a chase!
I wave at clouds, but they just drift,
Time's a present, but where's the gift?

At the café, I sip my tea,
A cupcake stares back, so tempting, see?
By the time I choose what's sweet,
The plate's empty, I can't compete!

The bus rolls by, I've missed the show,
Yet here I sit, enjoying the glow.
A fleeting laugh, a chance to play,
Guess I'll chase my dreams someday!

Moments fly, but I just grin,
Life's a whim, and so I spin!
Each second gone is just a tease,
I'll catch them all, just give me keys!

Endless Questions

Why are ducks the stars of parks?
Do they weave tales of noble larks?
Should I ask the squirrel on the wire?
Will it tell me, or just conspire?

What's the reason for a shoe?
Do they dance when I'm not in view?
With each inquiry, I feel so small,
Life's a riddle, can I solve it all?

Why do socks vanish into thin air?
Are they plotting with my missing hair?
Questions spin like leaves in wind,
Am I the one who's just been sinned?

I'll gather every oddball thought,
In a jar—but oh, I forgot!
Is the jar real, or just a jest?
Guess I'll ponder which is best!

Beneath the Surface of Familiarity

The couch knows all my lazy tricks,
Or do I just know its little kicks?
A creak here, and a pop there,
Is this comfort, or an affair?

I wander 'round my cluttered space,
Each hidden treasure has a face.
A dusty book begs for some love,
Is it wise, or just a shove?

Under the rug, a sock to find,
Oh sweet, it's the one that's blind!
Familiar corners hold a tale,
But are they fact, or just a fail?

I smile at quirks my treasure brings,
Silly secrets and funny flings.
In the comfort of what I know,
Funny things hide beneath the glow!

The Invisible Ink of Our Tales

Words float like whispers in the air,
Invisible tales, do they dare?
I spill my secrets on the floor,
But ink's not real? What's this for?

With stories shaped like silly hats,
I write of dogs and acrobats.
Yet blank pages start to tease,
Where went my muse? Oh, oh, jeez!

I scribble dreams of absurdity,
A penguin's dance? Oh can't you see?
The ink spills out through every crack,
Yet every glance, there's nothing back.

But in the silence, laughs ignite,
As tales emerge at the speed of light.
Invisible ink, you're such a prank,
In every giggle, let's find the bank!

Tides of Time and the Search for Answers

Waves come crashing, what a sight,
But where's my compass? Oh, that's right!
I walked that beach, so calm and grand,
Yet lost my keys, who needs a plan?

Seagulls squawk, they've got the flair,
But here I stand, a little bare.
I thought I knew which way to go,
Turns out, I should just ride the flow.

The tide rolls in, and so do doubts,
"Hey, wasn't that where fun's at?" shouts!
Is it the sand or my coffee spill?
At least I've learned, I can still thrill!

So grab your snacks and join the show,
The ocean's vast, our minds can grow.
We may not find the answers clear,
But laughter's the map, let's steer near!

Stargazing Beneath the Weight of Decisions

Stars are twinkling, what a view,
As I ponder which snack to chew.
Should it be chips or chocolate bars?
Oh, the burden of all these stars!

I asked the moon, for a little help,
It just chuckled, made me yelp!
"Flip a coin," it said with glee,
So I tossed it, fell asleep by the tree.

Planets align, or so they say,
But I can't find my other shoe today.
The constellations wink and nod,
At my journey, so very odd!

Decisions loom like clouds above,
Yet here I am, still dreaming of love.
With every sigh, I'll take a chance,
Who knew stargazing was a dance?

Timeworn Maps and New Beginnings

A map in hand, it's all unclear,
Is that a treasure or just a deer?
X marks the spot, but where's the gold?
Maybe it's chocolate, or so I'm told.

Old directions, they confuse the mind,
I end up lost, but oh, so blind.
The wind whispers, "Just take a stroll!"
As I trip over my own shoe pole.

An octopus waves with a friendly grin,
"Your joy is the map you've always been!"
But this old chart makes me sigh,
Perhaps I'll just fly a kite in the sky.

New paths to walk, adventures to find,
Who knew a map could be so maligned?
With laughter as guide, I'll take the chance,
For there's magic in a silly dance!

The Kaleidoscope of Purpose

Spinning shapes in a colorful turn,
What's the lesson? Oh, I discern!
Each twist reveals a laugh or two,
But still I ask, "What am I to do?"

The colors clash, they jive and play,
My purpose shifts every single day.
In patterns bright, I lose my way,
Yet somehow still, I feel okay.

Caught in this wondrous, silly glee,
Am I just a joke, or could it be?
The pie chart's wrong, it's round, not square,
Perhaps my purpose is just to share.

A twist, a twirl, let humor win,
For every purpose hides a grin.
In the kaleidoscope's endless sway,
I'll dance my way through each new day!

www.ingramcontent.com/pod-product-compliance
Lightning Source LLC
Chambersburg PA
CBHW071848160426
43209CB00003B/469